Tempus Fujitsu

Sotére Torregian
"L' Inconnu"
(The Unknown One)

***New and Late Poems and Writings

Arts & Letters Publishing — Madison, WI
ISBN: 978-1-961823-37-2
eBook ISBN: 978-1-961823-38-9
Title: *Tempus Fujitsu: "L' Inconnu" (The Unknown One)*
Author: Sotére Torregian
Digital distribution | 2025
Paperback | 2025

Dedication
(*Deducace*)

iii

This book is dedicated TO a mes amis de tante ans et d'ici encore
A Mme. Roseline Cleaver-Alric, Sherbrooke, Q.C.
Prof. Harry Cleaver émerité, Austin, Texas
AVANT mona mi avant
Et pour Mlles.Ondine et soeur Alicia
de la Liberté
Votre, S.T. ("l'Inconnu")
Surréalisme encore est CE QUE SERÀ
At moi Merci boucoup
Alors, je ne parle pias francaise je ne parle l'anglais je
ne parle pas le langage.
(Don't speak French don't speak English don't speak Language).

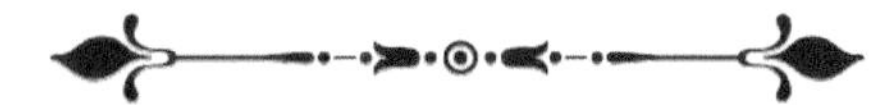

To Venture into Your Domain

With each new book....
I admit I am perplexed AS TO WHAT TO SAY about it as I am myself perplexed it as BUT then let the words freely flow where they may (André Breton, "Let the words make love") Thankful there are even words to set down or even type, As I say, GOOD MORNING to my typewriter…Again recalling it was Picasso who said, upon being asked the meaning of his work, "Let the works speak for themselves."

I must admit I was myself tempted to use that same statement in regard to my own writings, poems et al. but chose instead to shall I say – somewhat elaborate upon it, as I listened to the French composer, Erik Satie's GYMNOPEDIES, for which there is no rational explanation or meaning except to let the music, itself, captivating as it is, speak for itself and enchant the listener.

SO also for this ouvre, this book of mine, ever inspired by the words of Stéphane Mallarmé ('French poet, 1842—1898) "The Whole of the world exists to be made into a book translated from his prose piece, Quant au livre (Concerning the Book)

*(tout au monde existe pour aboutir à un livre)

The world exists to end in a book"

This has been my quest since I first put pen to paper, even from the beginning defying all existing literary conventions, to combine dream and reality sense and non-sense, Dadaistic black humor (umor noir) madness (la folie) and sanity (if such there be such a thing) words to scramble and re-scramble the puzzle of this our existence…

Recognizing André Branton (1896—1966) as my mentor, founder of surrealism, which I adopted as my way of life and career as a poet I cite, from his Surrealist Manifesto (English Translation) "Psychic automatism in its pure state" (defining the meaning of Surrealism) "by which one proposes—verbally, by means of the written word, or any other manner—the actual functioning of thought. Dictation of though, in the absence of any control whatsoever exercised by reason exempt from any aesthetic or moral concern."

I should add, parenthetically, *A Short Survey of Surrealism* by the poet David Gascoyne, who in 1936, introduced the English-speaking world to surrealist writing, poetry and art, in his own poems and essays.

These reference can be found in one's local library, for further study and illumination—as well as the Authors, own books of poetry and I add, immodestly, hereto).

-    Relevant if ever for today – and for this poet at least – in the upside-down in which we find ourselves.
                    —-Sotére Torregian (S.T.)
                    20 August 2023

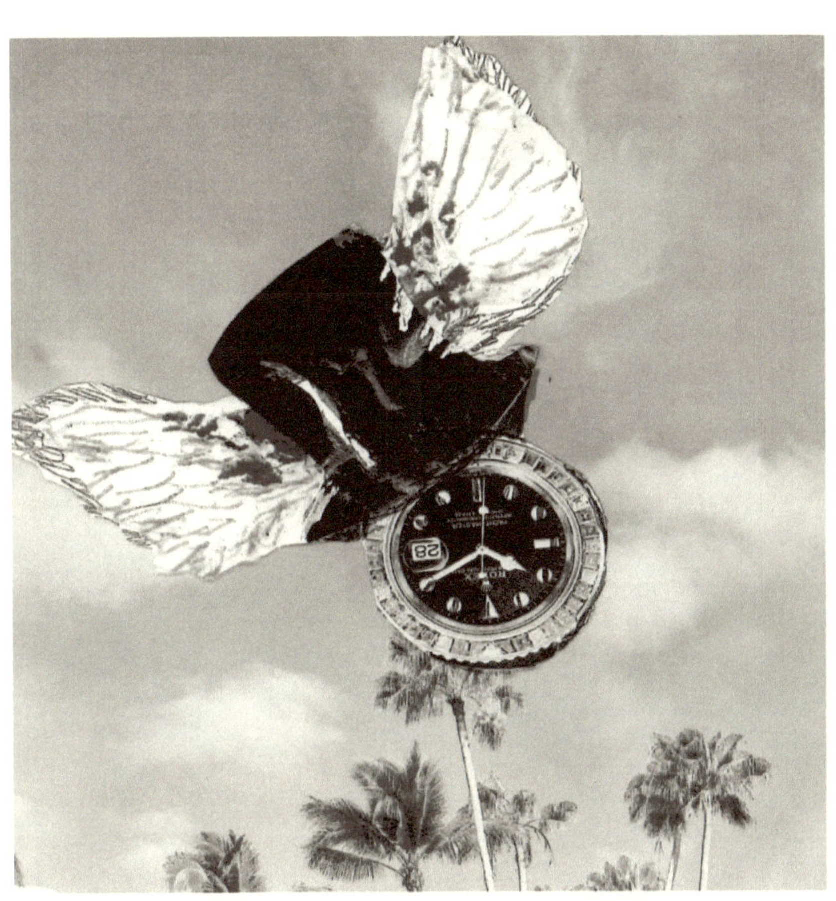

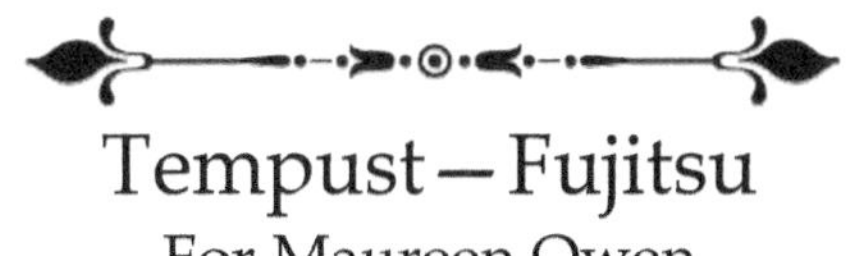

Tempust — Fujitsu
For Maureen Owen

Comme un plain-chante mais non comme une berceuse malenké
— L.S. Sebghor, Lettres d' hivernage

BY WAY OF
Connecticut and New York
And M. Heisenberg's UNDERTAINTY PRINCIPLE
Red Berrigan's serenading a bottle of Pepsi
Jomo Kenyatt's Kenyan fly-swater as scepter
You found yourself FULLY YOU
Not being assessed or having to run the gauntlet through Silicon
Valley's intimidating Execs to qualify for "A Girl Friday"
YOU FOUND YOURSELF A FULLY INTACT A WOMAN
— As Patrick Stewert (Of Star Strek Fame)

Now reads a Shakespeare Sonnet for each day
Bearing Witness —-For the reality of our being (l' ester)
AS I roam rootless
restless throughout the course
Of the day

YET AM URGED
By the Ambuscado Of The Poem
As I am awakened each night
TO MY OWN NAME AND IDENTITY
AS I REMEMBER YOU
AT 2 A.M.

      —- S.T.
     February, 2020

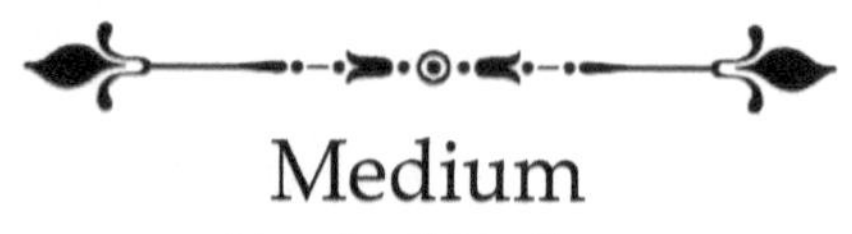

Medium
For Joel Dailey

Non couer est un coucou pour Dieu
– André Breton, Claire de Terre

While waiting for
Yet another glimpse of Vanna White's legs on T.V
(Wheel of Fortune)
I never know what I'm doing these days
I know, for certain though
I'm not Chief Yellow Knife, but rather Abd at-Rahman
Writing a love poem in Exile the Charmin Bears
About to sing 8 PM Wednesday how did this come about?
I don't know
what musical note corresponds to
according to Father Gurjieff's scale of
the soul's ladder "On a scale of one to ten" then
I don't which one I've reached at the moment
How many times
will you write
the date of the old year in place of the current (2020)

"Slow but steady wins the race"
Linda Ronstadt says the Tortoise to the Hare
Ah, a stalactite on my bed
It 8s too late I've missed her again this time
AS now the animals begin habitation of Winter
Gabrielle Gallimbert
Children were proud to show their toys
whether they were many or few
DISCONNECT

Volodymyr Zelensky's Comedy of Errors
But Missed
Beethoven's 249 Birthday Party

S.T
December 18th, 2019

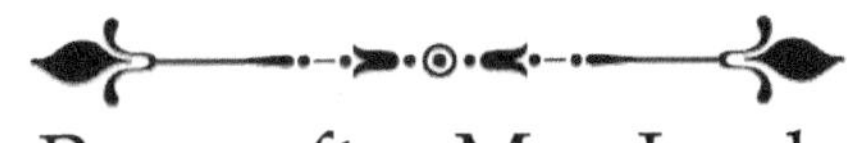

Poem after Max Jacob
For Maxine Groffsky

The three dames who play the bugle
take baths late into the night in their bathrooms
they have for master a certain dullard
who's only there before noon.
The little blond boy catching crabs
the crabs grasped right in his hands
says not a word
he's a child born out of adultery.
Three mothers for this bald kid
One would have been enough
The dad's a nabob but poor
treats him like a dog
(<u>Signed</u> —-)
<u>Choir of Muses you bedazzle me</u>
<u>IT'S me</u> you see playing on the bugle
on the Jena Bridge on Sundays
wearing a signboard on his sleeve
(that says "Indigent")

Translation from the French,
S.T. 1965

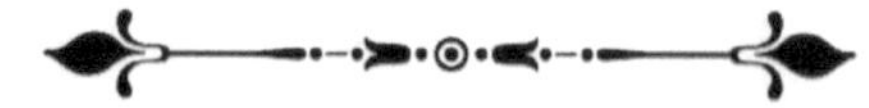

Foodtown (Newark, New Jersey)
For Joe and Rose Ceravolo

I can't quite catch up now while
holding this bag of groceries
coming home O City of broken glass
bottlenecks! My right hand
thinner than my left try this
just for size.
Boys with broomsticks
dogs coming out of chimneys
yards leading to unspeakable promise
bandaged windows trees verbose branches
Adonis coming out of the building.
Ahhh
tonsils we can't escape as usual
Cracked sidewalks!
Doesn't pay to get hit by a swerving taxi-cab
it appears the woman passenger inside
will be late for the delivery room
Broken god-king of ceilinged fire

S.T.
circa 1965

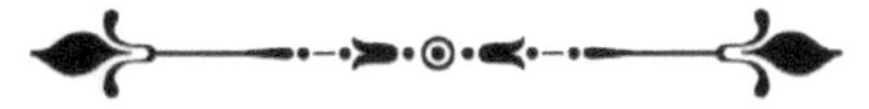

For Tom Clark in France
For Tom and Angelica Clark

This part of the year my wife's face appears as an
Illumined Garden Diner. It will be colder at night
to print. Sometimes caffeine in an older October converts
the tonic acid. One cup may not poison a drinker.
BUT clearly aging Green tea city of witches shafts the chalice
Paved on top of the veins of ore prominent Into which
I walk like a Protestant Jesus with fluorescence
Dear umbrellas bring. Theatrical spongewood castanets cymbals
high
medium and low Chinese blocks — This is the very luster dissipating
the essential mortgage, the fowling projector
filming its own obsequies the very eaglestone running
Now you know our harsh Twin City electrocutions of the jumper's
gift
of absolute pitch, its lingo the nun's beach
"Either a man or a wall"

S.T.
May-June, 1966

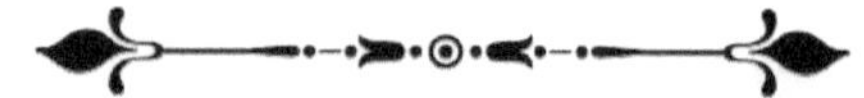

On the Knocking at the Door in Macbeth
For Anne (Waldman)

Six o'clock
I smell the beach
without the beach
Six o'clock
I smell the beach
without the Beach
Six o'clock.
I smell the beach
without the beach.

     —Sotére Torregian
     Summer, 1969

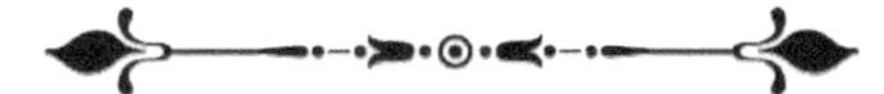

For Ted Joans Tombouctou
(1928-2003)

"I've been kissed by a beautiful woman"
L'Ocean de l'aventure se transforms en desert où le
poéte ne peut voir que sa propre image"
— Héléne Larouche Davis, Robert Deanos, Une Voix
un chant un cri

Whowas I what will I be a star a fish
a grenade. How is it that
tears issue so readily did I once so
tread their porcelain stair of the entropic
palace as emissary or king
And what am I to bring
in the advance
of your name falconry derailment
or a caravan
of trumpets blaring
tributaries of Akkadian cuneiform
the telephone of the one demon-possessed
woman isn't ringing while I play
gold with "snapbacks" crawling in from the cracks
And at the same time
tale my fists in the shadow of Lenin haranguing
the masses all of which is a necessary
composite of my being (l' etre)
ANNOUNC INSURRECTION of Des Noirs
displacing the code of Americus Vespucci all the way
from L.A. to the Pelham Park Expressway
Who was I what will I be in Meadow Lark
Crude oil demask or offertory.
Note: Ted Joans, (1928-2003) Afro-American Surrealist Poet,
Friend, spent time between Paris and Timbuktu (Fr. Sp.
Tombouctou) San Fransisco, New York and Los Angeles. Coffee
House Press published his definitive oeuvre
Teducation in 1999.

S.T.
30 May, 1992

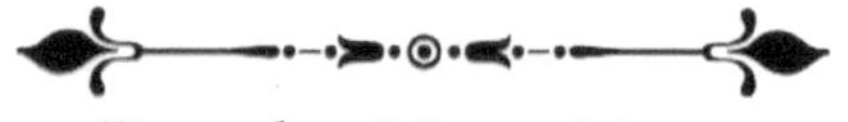

For the New Year
For Maureen Owen

SOUS les alphabets incomprehensibles du moment
— Aime Cesaire, Noria

I'm looking for a poem for the New Year
Perhaps a Chinese poet wrote it
Exploded with fireworks in Beijing
Perhaps a Martian wrote it
(but they don't celebrate New Years' on Mars)
I know I'll eventually have to face an audience
And someone there will inevitably ask
"Do you have a poem for the New Year?"
And I won't know what to say.
Actually surreptitiously I could very well crib
from Max Jacob (always a good reliable source)
But that won't do
Now I've spelt diarrhea incorrectly
(always leave out the second "R")

As for the entry for today in my journal
The bottle of champagne anxiously awaits
in the fridge there's music going on in there
a Due Cori
played by an invisible orchestra
the music stops however when I open the door to the fridge
The Northern Lights momentarily flare in there

S.T.
le Janvier d' l' an 2015

Automatiques
Pour Mme. Denise Warmerdam

The shadow of my hand at 3 A.M. swims
as a fluid fish in a moment
then disappears in my grasp as I move
about the room unsettled yet still half-asleep
It will be in a matter of hours
before high-heels will clatter to begin
resounding the pinioned cycle
of the workday week
The ink of my pen flows smoothly
across the blank page
If my hand could only now reach
out to where you are as I roam bedraggled
here drunk before any drink has touched my lips
My own boyhood Assassin appears
 before me as peering out at me
from the mirror as an egress I assume
the presence of the Thief of Baghdad
to thrust myself into an unsuspecting princes boudoir
Yet find I remain shipwrecked here (naufragée)
still maintain in the din of ensuing chores
in the onset of contending hours

S.T.
—mars (March) 2016

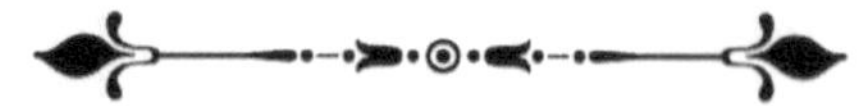

Disclosure: the Velcro Manual

I snooze through the news—ooze
We're out of place here
Like John Wayne titling the piano -keys
a -le Thelonius Monk at the Five Spot (N.Y.C.)
Thought it was hopeless at the time
to interpret
But then MR. A.A. Antipyrene appears on the screen
acting as Nuncio
"We are honored you have decided to protector our identity"
And given the opportunity afforded there's absolutely
no reason why not to write poetry
to appease the faraway stars in heaven
Or, then, the silence in the Rain Forest
Then, again, the clouds of Prince Andrei gazed at fallen
from his mount at Austerlite
GIVE US a mandate then
to Boycott Chick-Fil-A's across the country!
For the chickens who can't speak
for themselves nor take up arms across the Carnivore oppressor
Clocks
would Strike at the hour in sympathy in a Walk-Out
leave their positions at GOOGLE
—A flame-thrower *FUG word aimed at Wall Street just in
"Real Time Numbers"
"Too much glue and not enough white-out"

Sorére Torregian and Collin Schuster
November, 2017

Notes of Mr. A.A. Antipyrene by Tristan Tzara, a Dadaist epic FUG word. The "Fugs" event-garde songsters (Ted Berrigan, Tuli Kupherberg and Ed Sanders, poets) organized a troupe and recoded songs, New York 1966—1967

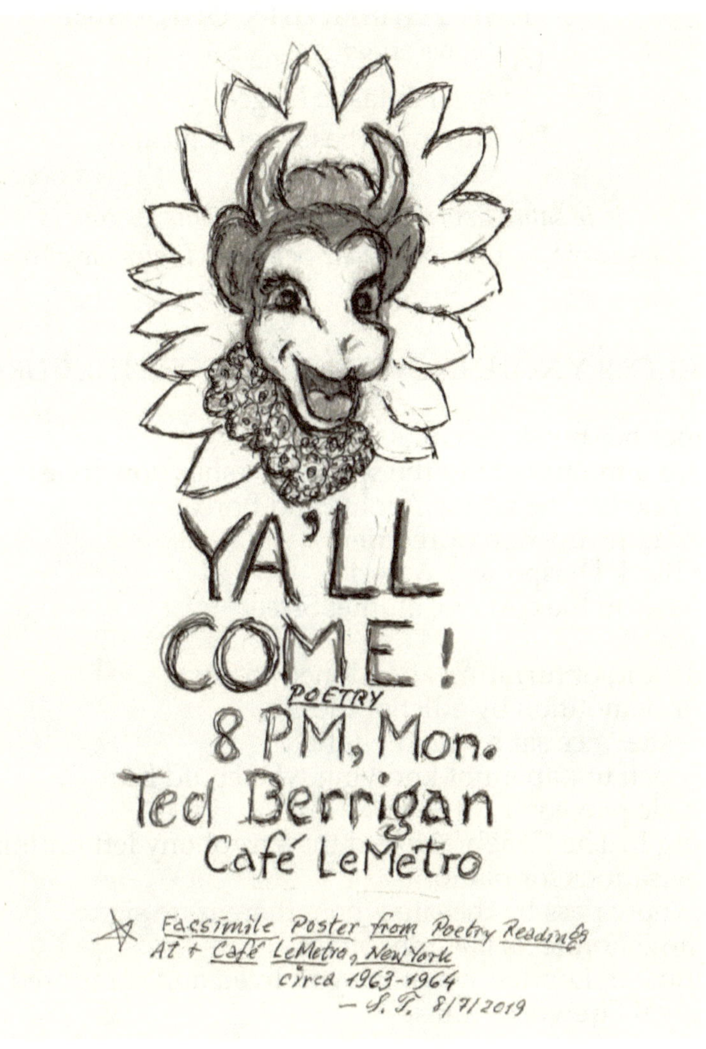

Facsimile Poster from Poetry Readings
At † Café LeMetro, New York
circa 1963-1964
— S. T. 8/7/2019

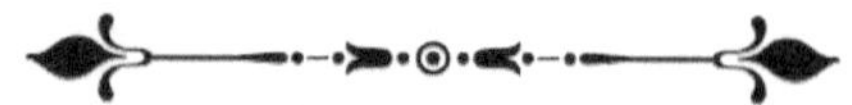

Miss Florence Price
African American Composter
(April 9th, 1887 – June 3rd, 1953)
Fantastic Négre
To: Calvin Forbes, Poet, Chicago

Je te salue Esprit qui t' incarnes dens les couers
les corps – -Léoplold Sédar Senghor, Élgies mejeures

WHERE ONLY NOTES NOW DANCE BEFORE THE CURLICUED
STAFF
on paper her music remains
There as a monument to the spirit her ashes now long
consecrated to the winds Aeolus and Boreas
sans extreme unction or requiem
In the Black Diaspora of America
the house on the corner Calumet Street
in Chicago
now devoid of furniture abandoned to dust
due for demolition by edict of the city
Where she once sat by candlelight
setting pen to paper not knowing who could hear
her music played
Dancing In The Canebrake and the symphony left unfinished
improvisations for piano…
People now pass by the site where there is no sign
to commemorate its late inhabitant
The home in London where Haydn lived and composed
The Royal Fireworks music
now visited by tourists worldwide
Or the Salzburg of Mozart…
The Mozarteum dedicated to his memory
Chopin's apartment in Paris – The Great Migration Northward that
bestirred
Langston Hughes, Zora Neale Hurston – The Harlem Renaissance
O genius inherited of Mandangue richness of poetry and song

Transplanted through shackles and blood
the four-hundred-year legacy of Forebearers
Her images in sound yet survive in the Noösphere
Of Spirit (and graciousness)

<u>Of William Grant Still</u>
<u>–her Heir apparent and Oracle Et mon homage, Madame,</u>
<u>encore</u>
–S.T.
April, 2019

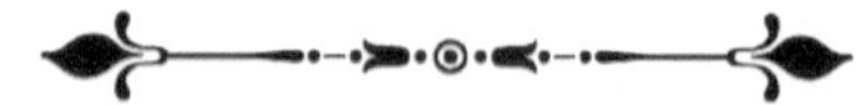

Uncollected No Name Uno
For Patricia Biddle, R.N. And Joel Dailey, Fell Swoop

Un lac de mais fauve flaire par acre vent
— Aimé Césaire, Noria

On the road to the fog-overcast hospital
Where I'm magic-carpeted
Further! -Plus Loin Will bring the map
you hadn't known
To this of No Name Uno
(Township Of) (Gilroy famed for its Garlic Festival)
Where I'm trundled and hoised
It's no use here trying to hold up a box in place
Days hours rolled into one. Sickbay Lost Weekend
As long as there's a pen in my pocket but can't find
Fuck my gown's upside down for this je-suis-mal nuptial!
In the fine linen of the hour
Perhaps you've never been
face-a-face to the type face of a poem
But perhaps
Dear lady the childhood memory of a
Shakespearean sonnet lies still
lingering there somewhere in your
breast undisclosed
O to reach it
that tympanium where you are
Near but unreachable incalculable incognito'd
moments away from my sight
The two-point conversion
to make a field-goal amongst all these wires
hooked-up I.V. tubes encircling me like the Bulls of Bushin
defeated in this joust
unhorsed ancient knight it's a fitting theme
For the forlorn drifting along with the Tumbling Tumbleweed

Yet am made comfortable ensconced and confident (Somewhat)
by your dulcet words
patting down my pillow into a cloud
as you do so hovering nearby waiting
for your returning touch

                          —Sotère Torregian
                          —November 26-29, 2019
                          Morgan Hill, California

At the Mirror Feeling a Bit Groggy…
For my Friend, poet Frank Lima (1939 – 2013)

O , trompa à mon sècours Je me suis ègare par le foret de ses cheveux
— Leopold Sedare Senghor, Nocturnes (– 433)

At the mirror still feeling a bit groggy this morning
I cut myself shaving
I remembered
your beardless face looking almost Roman
as you welcomed me in your apartment
your lovely lady Vogue Model Shayla Baykal seated there
I had been wandering in the fog of New York City
(1966) the City become a labyrinth
I didn't know where to go or what to do
In love with my Carmen-Therèse sixteen-year-old water nymph
who'd left me to go off to L.A.
 Feeling shattered I didn't even remember your Apt. No.
Or what street I was travelling in
but somehow found my way to your place
lost in a daze our of the labyrinth
I don't remember what I said that night
as you sat me down at your table and offered me a "stiff drink"
to brace me up.
But your words were spare and kind
as your charged me to go forth again
and make a new poem out of my miserere
to go forth!
This seemingly late word of Thanks
— And to find love yet again restored in the world

—S.T.
June, 2018

The Longest Day and Night of the Year
(Winter Solstice, Dec. 21st 2019)

A river runs through it till Burnham Wood
do god knows where to and fro
North Shore Animal League America/Michigan
And Astoria Southern Russia
Where Tolstoy spent his last days
Which I don't want to think about
The Yangstee and would feel Bard's witchy work
the fingers of the world seek answers
si seuliment il fasait soleil cette nuit
If only the sun made this night
The curtain-fall on the horizon
What was Seurat doing here
speaking of red halos surrounding green foliage
O Messajero nestegg allow
I don't know who these women are
here dressed in discalced monk's robes
Topical Analgesic sic semper tyrannis
Above the bedcovers dance the Symplegades again
the approach the sea has brought nothing to us
but feathers of Montezuma's headdress
It happens our own presence here is measured
life in the Earthly Paradise or not
of Nikki Jabber's Garden in Hallifax
"Nobody dies"
Sever cheers ado Trafalgar Square
O solitary orphanage inside myself
scion of Prometheus
Will remembrance go through
still rekindle fire?

S.T.
December 23, 2019

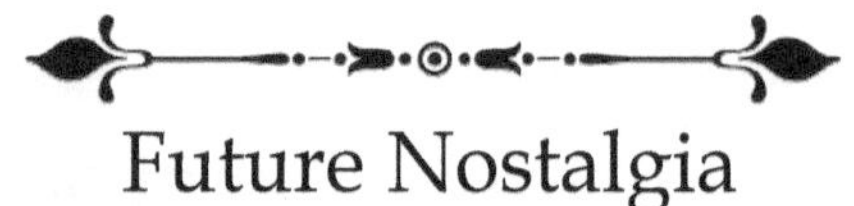

Future Nostalgia

l' amour present et l'avenir
le poida du monde
— Tristan Tzara, De memoire d' homme (1392)

Along roads heading nowhere
There's a town near Santa Fe called Fooliah Talk
where Bollywood films are made
Throwing a snowball at the Barber of Seville
with a great report-card
O bathwater tester
Descadent in Teen-speak "No Stomo"
As we are proine to lose our way and wander
in the void to Flora's Fields
melting into one another
Anadante Spinato'd amongst other high points
where elephants gather to give us lessons on etiquette
Where shadows gather in waiting
THERE IS NO FUTURE
Nor Past
The Future is only NOW as I blow my nose
its whoosh Nynquam
*No longer past tense what) as oppose
to Forecasters of doom de dee dee da
Where I can't embrace you
in London once the ancient Londonium
Londonium — who knew! To what end
The so-called "Future" we all embrace and traversed
in the Valley of the Blind
no need to consult the Riemann Hypothesis
What the saints have always
unmasked and told us for countless years
and poets continue to unmask the charade of nostalgia
As the future so-called which is now.

S.T.
Sometime in 2020

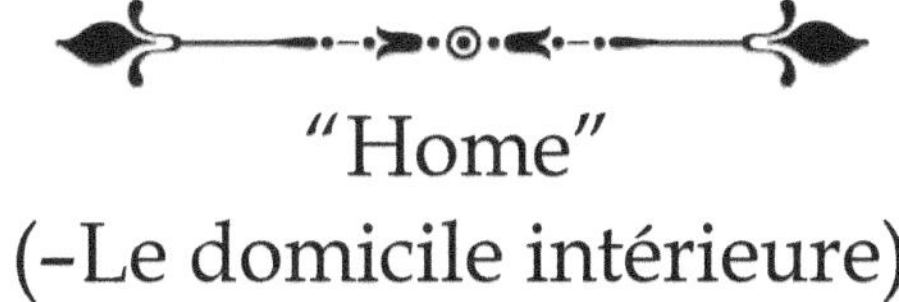

"Home"
(–Le domicile intérieure)

"je suis appuye contre un mur svac des oreilles verdoyantes"
— Paul Eluard

What "home" as the poet (Andre Frenaud) says, there is only a
real home in poetry.
There no one comes knocking on the door (secret police) or a
landlord demanding his rent.
No invading armies of bull collectors.
To this "home" I have given Rachmaninoff the key to enter at
any time…Or, for that matter Schubert or Back as guests.
A balalaika or a piano?
Painters are welcome here, Miro or Matiese
The silence that surrounds this internal home.
The memory of a beautiful woman once loved.
The Silk Road with its dromedaries and caravansaries
also finds its way here.
Time may go forward or stop here.
The only treasure to be found hidden here is that of l' esprit
the spirit that he's moved every artist or poet from time immemorial
At the entrance to this domicile is the dream-catcher of
the Lakota Indians (Native Americans) which allow only good dreams
to enter. None of the acquisition or power over others.
And yes finally inevitably, words, les mots. On their journey
I myself may be lost but the stars tell me I still have a home within.
Dens mon inttérieure

December, 2020
Stockton, California

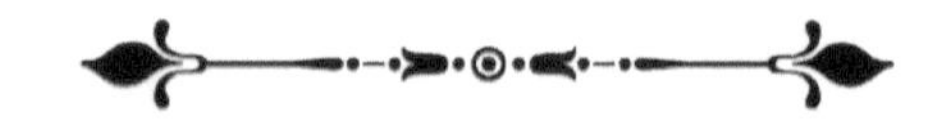

Mr. Strauss' Claim to Fame

Court Detective
Museum Piece
Complicated, so to Speak
Star Voice in UP
Stone worker
Eats at a banquet
Extended Stories
Spiral Shell
Baseball Great Wade
Chicken portion
Casino Command
Harmonize with
Prepares for Casting
Appears ominously
American living in
Athens
Pointless

S.T.
9. Ix. 2020

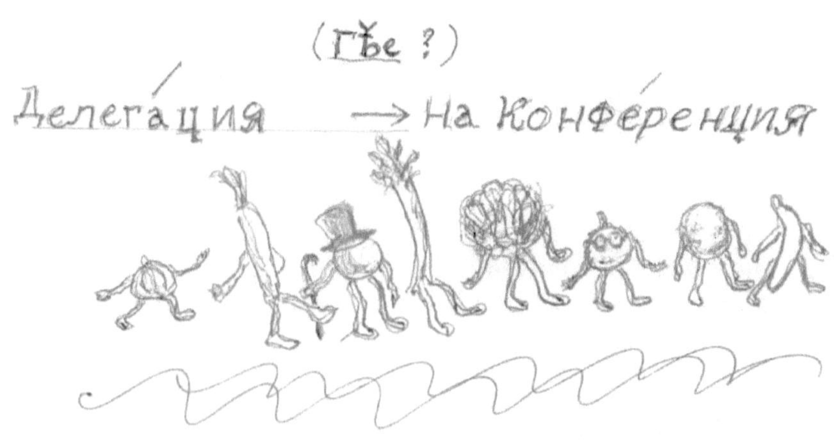
(Гдѣ ?)
Делега́ция ⟶ На Конфере́нция
Whereunto?
(Russ. trans
) Whereunto? The Delegati on Off To A Conference
S.T. 2019

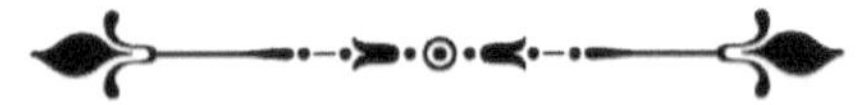

On a Line from Elio Schneeman
(1961 – 1996)

Ourvrir les portes quoi qu' on ait, ne sont pas de celles
terirent si vainment

"I am That Madman" opened at random
and found myself in your line
The one you spoke of in "Along the Rails"
Although we never met
I am reminded each time
of my own desolation and madness
The piano concerto no.2 I've heard
so many times in my life before
Possibly it was the first time at age 3 (?)
it doesn't matter if it became thematic hereafter
for me the hunger of Being in the world
Perhaps it was then when the nurse touched my
naked body or was it?

When I recognized my prototype in the
and thus found myself thereafter walking
beside André Breton's doppelgänger
on a street in downtown Newark (NJ)
(although the poet was still in Paris)
Thereupon my "second birth" ensued
the problem remained what to do with this
madness.
How to transform the world
with it or ride into oblivion

S.T.
2020

"A Rescusant Actor"
(New York 1962 — 1967)
A Memoire for Ms. Evelyn Cabral
In mem. Joe Ceravolo (1934 — 1988)

And the lips still lock onto lips
and the arms still link and reach out
to embrace
The Other

(Where I am now devoid here and now of)
2nd Avenue and East 9th St. and the Café LeMetro
become a Chinese Laundry and there are no more
readings by poets at 1 P.M. Wednesday night where and when

I first made a furtive debut before having a quaffed a draught
of Wild Turkey proffered by my friend Paul Blackburn
as we waited out entrance from the freezing cold
by the café door for it to be opened finally
to smell of steaming express and a sign-in on the roster
The trip on the No. 118 Bus in the afternoon
from Newark N.J. to Manhattan the view of the city
skyline in anticipation to be in another world of dreams
away from the daily grind and hucksterism
(of the neighborhood Little Catania and Nicosia)
of my immigrant origins and glowering relatives
There was the first sight of freedom I ever knew
No need to show an I.D. or pass an exam to prove myself
or jump hurdles into nothingness placed there by
society and its angst and grasp

S.T.
2020

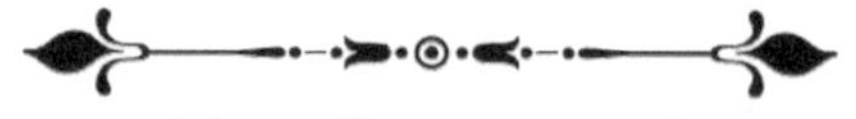

(Au Contraire)
There is No "Brain Revolution"
For Maria Schriver, Inc.

IT NEVER HAPPENED in the laboratories
IT IS ALL AS THEY USED TO SAY "Wolf Cookies," a q.v., the media
It can't come without the auctioneers selling their tickets to the show.
Ask the owls and turtles who hold the real secret from which humans
are left out. It is only the elephant who holds the real secret
in its brain.
Perhaps the walnut's enclosed and it's there?
A song-and-dance for the pharmaceuticals promo
Perhaps in the soup vindaloo but no.
Alas, Perhaps if I sleep with my saddle-bags
under the stars, I'll find…the answer your goon-faced
doctors know nothing
But it's true inside you the Cracker-Jack box on the ferris-wheel
Whatever's there will keep spinning
Without you knowing
Without you discovering
Without you Chicago-que — Madame
It's perhaps in the ceremony
of the Apache Devil-Dance
I will never know

S.T.
2020

www.ingramcontent.com/pod-product-compliance
Lightning Source LLC
Chambersburg PA
CBHW022045050726
47591CB00003B/959